Under The Stone

Early Women Doctors in Evergreen Cemegery

Doris A McCraw

Contents

Additional Copyright and Contact Information

Chinook Mountain Publishing – Colorado Springs, Colorado

For more information, or to book an event, contact:

ChinookMountainPublishing@gmail.com

Photographs by: Doris A. McCraw

Cover design by Doris A. McCraw

First Edition: August 2022

Acknowledgements

THIS BOOK WOULD NOT be without the help of a community of people who also share the joy of history. I must thank Chris Nichol, who encouraged me to start putting down the information I so passionately researched. The Special Collections Department of the Pikes Peak Library District which houses so many wonderful resources. Abby Mall, with Evergreen Cemetery, who helped by finding old documents that allowed me to find the resting places of these amazing women.

I also want to thank my friends who continued to encourage me to follow through and continue to tell the stories of these women, Dianne Hartshorn, Liz Duckworth, Patricia Willis Kemp, and so many others. Thank you all.

Chapter Three

Author's Note to the Readers

IN RESEARCHING THE STORY of these amazing women every effort has been made to verify their information. As new information becomes available, some facts may vary.

In telling the story of both Julia E. Loomis and Harriett Leonard, both have family stories that place them in Colorado Springs by 1876.

Documents do verify their presence in the Pikes Peak Region in 1878.

Regardless, telling the story of these women is something that is important to the history of this region. Look at this as a start, rather than the definitive information.

Doris A. McCraw

Chapter Four

Introduction

Evergreen Cemetery, like the city it was created for, is full of adventures, dreamers and pioneers. Of those early settlers, a number were women doctors. These early medical pioneers came to the region to use their gifts and knowledge to help cure or at least ease the suffering of the health seekers who flocked to the region. A number of the women who arrived before 1900 moved on, but some stayed, sharing their lives and knowledge with the city. Their resting place is here in the silence of the cemetery. We should honor them, remembering what we can find of their lives.

Chapter Five

Medicine In The 1800s

At the time these women were practicing their chosen profession, medicine is not the same we see practiced today. Women were beginning to make headway in the medical field. Elizabeth Blackwell, in 1849, was the first woman to graduate medical school in the United States. During the Civil War, despite the willingness to help out, women doctors were excluded from serving. Dr. Mary Edwards Walker was determined to serve. She became a 'contract acting assistant surgeon', the first woman U. S. Army surgeon, even earning a pension.

The medical profession was much different from what we know today. A person could become a doctor by paying a practicing physician for the privilege to study with them as Dr. Harriot Kezia Hunt did in 1830s in Boston. They could also attend a medical college for two years. At the time women started attending medical college the length of study was two years, without prior college or even a high school education. The courses were not for the feint of heart, and study they did, learning the latest practices, in their chosen type of medicine.

Prior to 1900, there were three major types of medical practice. The primary was homeopathy, followed by allopathy, then osteopathy. Of the four earliest women doctors in the region, three were homeopaths.

To perhaps better understand, here are some very simple definitions of the three terms as used in the late nineteenth century.

Homeopathy is the concept that disease is treated with minute amount of 'drugs' that create the same symptoms as the disease and therefore using the bodies ability to fight off illness. Homeopathy originated in 1796 in Germany. Its basic tenant is like cures like. In 1844 the American Institute of Homeopathy was founded on the east coast, the first medical association of any kind in the United States. Its purpose; promote and standardize the practice and teaching of this modality of medicine.

Allopathy is the idea that you treat the disease using 'drugs' from outside the body which would be in opposition to the symptoms and that would produce the desired wellness. (Most M. D.'s in practice today would have been known as allopaths). In the 1800s think of bleeding, and leeches, for early allopaths. In later years it was cocaine, arsenic, and mercury until further discoveries. Although a smallpox vaccine had been discovered in 1799, antibiotics among other modern therapies had not yet been discovered.

Osteopathy, which began in 1874, is the idea that the bones in the body structure were the starting point from which a 'condition' arose and emphasized the treatment of medical disorders through the manipulation and massage of the bones, joints, and muscles.

One unique modality to the United States was the Eclectic practice. The basic premise was using what was available in the region, much like indigenous peoples had done. The focus was on botanicals and physical therapies.

Chapter Six

The Pikes Peak Region

SO WHAT BROUGHT THESE women to the Pikes Peak Region so early in its development? No definitive answer has been found, but there are pieces of information that lead to an educated guess.

From the regions earliest days the climate was always a part of the discussion of the Pikes Peak Region, Colorado Springs and

Manitou Springs in particular. From the earliest city directory and newspapers, they write about the moderate climate and its benefit to health.

The following, found in the 1879-80 Colorado Springs City Directory, seems a standard description of the region:

"The altitude of Colorado Springs, 6000 feet above the level of the sea, it's protection in a great measure from the north and west winds, by the divide on the North and the mountain range on the west, render the climate of this locality one of the most salubrious and delightful to be found in the world. It's altitude and proximity to the mountains temper the summer heat, the nights during that season being always cool enough for comfort. During the autumn and winter months the atmosphere is dry and invigorating with an almost uninterrupted sunshine. But little rain falls during the autumn and none in the winter, and usually snowfall is confined to the spring months when the ground being warm, it soon melts away. Thousands of invalids of all classes flock hither and to Manitou, and nearly all find relief from their respective ailments, while very many, particularly those suffering from asthma, throat and lung troubles, dyspepsia and general debility, are permanently cured."

The directory continues with this description of Manitou Springs. "The town of Manitou, celebrated for its soda and iron springs, is located in a beautiful glen among the mountains, at the very foot of Pike's Peak...In the summer season Manitou is thronged with health and pleasure seekers from all parts of the United States and Europe. During the season of 1878, which was unusually short, 5651 visitors registered at the several hotels. Owing to its thorough protection from the winds, Manitou is a favorite winter resort for invalids...

The mineral springs which have given to this locality a worldwide popularity are eight in number... Comparison is made with the waters of the celebrated springs at Spa, in Belgium..." Dr. Samuel Edwin Solly, an English doctor who arrived in hopes of curing him and his wife, who wrote extensively on the benefits of climate on health.

The region as a mecca for health seekers also made it a destination for the doctors who wished to cure the diseases plaguing the population at the time. It also brought the charlatans, magicians, and other con men and women who played upon the desperation of those same health seekers. The women included in this book all were graduates of a medical college and earned their M.D, designation or were licensed by the state of Colorado. They are all but forgotten and it is the hope the book you have in your hands will remedy that oversight. Here are the stories of those early, courageous women now resting in Evergreen Cemetery.

Julia E. Loomis-Headstone

JULIA E. LOOMIS

Julia E. Loomis – Base of her Headstone

Block 40

Julia E. Loomis

JULIA **E. LOOMIS** WAS the first woman doctor who was a medical college graduate in Colorado Springs. One early source says she arrived here as early as 1876. While that may or may not be the case, she definitely was here in 1878. Her ad in the August 1878 Gazette read, "Mrs. J. E. Loomis, M. D. Special attention given to diseases of women and children. Residence corner of Tejon and Kiowa Street."

Julia was born on January 16, 1816,. to Samuel and Polly Frizell of New Woodstock, New York the youngest of ten daughters. (There were fourteen children born to this union) On January 7, 1836, Julia married J.C. (John) Loomis. They remained in New York state, during the early years of their marriage. Both of their children were born there. A son, John Lewis Loomis b.1838, and a daughter, Julia Gertrude Loomis, b.1844.

In 1856 Julia, John, and their family moved west to Washington Township, Buchanan County, Iowa.

The town of Independence, founded in 1847, was the county seat. Their daughter, Gertrude, married Charles W. Taylor on May 22, 1861, in Buchanan County at the age of 18. Three years later on April 1, 1864, at the age of 21, Gertrude died. She is buried in Independence Iowa.

Although their son John Lewis Loomis did not live with the family, he also took up residence in Independence, Iowa at around the same time. He and his wife Alice M. Loomis had a son, Linn born on December 26, 1868, but died on January 7, 1869. Linn is buried in Oakwood cemetery, Independence,

Iowa. John was the editor of the 'Bulletin' in 1865 but sold it the following year. He also served as postmaster until 1880 when he, Alice, and their family moved to Colorado. They had two other children, Melvin born around 1870, and Gertrude born around 1872.

Julia attended the Cleveland Woman's Homeopathic College, a homeopathic school, where she graduated with her M. D., in February of 1870 at the age of fifty-four. From there she and John moved to McMinnville, Warren County, Tennessee. During 1872-73 she spent some time in Atlanta, Georgia, and returned during the early part of 1876. An ad in the 'Atlanta Constitution' during that time read in part "Mrs. Loomis not only attends to general practice, but gives special attention to CHRONIC DISEASES of every description, in which, as well as Obstetrics she has had marked success".

After Julia and her husband John arrived in Colorado Springs, she set up her medical practice. This was at a time when many 'doctors' were arriving in the area. Dr. Boswell P. Anderson was the first physician in Colorado Springs. A Veteran of the Civil War, serving in the 43rd Virginia Calvary Company D. from January 1863- April 1865, Anderson spent most of his career treating tuberculous. For a time, he and Dr. Solly had a practice together in Colorado Springs. There were also a number of what we would call, quacks, who arrived, many of who called themselves doctors but had neither the qualifications nor certificate to prove their worth.

Julia continued her chosen profession until her death on March 12, 1880, of pneumonia. She was sixty-four years old. Her death certificate was signed by Dr. Esther B. Holmes.

This excerpt from Julia's address to her fellow classmates/graduates, published in the Cleveland Daily

Herald on March 3, 1870, sums up the sentiment of these early pioneering female physicians:

"Long having had a desire to acquire a knowledge of the practice of medicine, and the door being opened, I entered this college nearly ignorant of all leading branches connected with the science, in one sense like a child, yet with more than a child's desire to learn. But now as I go out from among you, may I not hope to go prepared to some extent, at least to relieve the suffering of my own sex, and also to bear the responsibility pertaining to our position. Reference having been made to the trifling value of a diploma allow me to think otherwise. As I go out into this new field of action, I can take this roll in my hand, as I come in contact with opposition I can use it as a shield of defense. It may therefore be considered as a token of great value to everyone who shall fill this useful and honorable profession."

Harriet A. Leonard - Headstone

Harriet Leonard

Block 58

Harriet A. Leonard

HARRIET **A LEONARD** WAS different from Julia Loomis but how? What were Harriett's background and education? She was also born in New York. She attended the Keokuk School of Physicians and Surgeons, an allopathic school, in Keokuk, Iowa. This school was a very early state-funded co-ed school in the United States.

The school medical school was originally located in LaPorte, Indiana. In 1849, the school moved to Keokuk and began classes in November 1850. The school was, according to an article in the 1927 Journal of the Iowa State Medical Society, "nominally the medical department of the State University of Iowa, recognized as such by the Iowa legislature". The State University of Iowa was located in Iowa City, Iowa, ninety-five miles north of Keokuk. As a result of this association, when the University became the first publicly supported university to be co-educational in 1870, the school in Keokuk, by mandate had to accept female students into the medical program.

Harriet Adams married John J. Leonard on September 6, 1846, in Michigan. He was living in Hillsdale, Hillsdale County, Michigan, and Harriet was living in Calvin Township, Cass County, Michigan at the time of their union.

An early mention of Dr. Leonard appears in the Pueblo paper in 1876, with no mention of her location. In the 1877 Denver City Directory she and her husband John, a miller, are listed with the address of 274 20th street. She is listed as a physician. Dr. Alida Avery, who had arrived in Denver in

1874 is also listed in the directory and yet neither is listed among the thirty-two male physicians in that category. The couple also is in the 1886-1889 Denver City Directories.

From 1877 through 1886 Dr. Leonard was in Manitou Springs. Her ads begin appearing in the 1878 Gazette. One ad, from July 1878 read as follows: "Mrs. H. A. Leonard M.D. Electrician. special attention given to nervous and chronic diseases. office in the mineral bath house. Manitou."

Dr. Leonard was a proprietor of a bathhouse, not something many people saw a woman doing. The thing about Dr. Leonard she appeared to be learning and applying those lessons to her work. there is some indication she traveled to hot springs, New Mexico, although no definitive documentation has been found. it would not be out of the question, hot springs, now truth or consequences, New Mexico, was a place of numerous hot springs. the springs in Manitou are mineral and were used mostly for drinking to get the benefits.

Harriet Leonard seemed to never give up. in 1891 she established a Russian vapor and electric bath at 21 North Tejon. she had two assistants, one male and the other female, both expert masseurs and she guaranteed scientific treatment. in 1892 she spoke about her plan to build a wood and stone sanitarium on her Washington Ave property.

in the 1900 census, Harriet is a widow, her husband John having passed in 1895/6. this census also showed the couple had had seven children, with four still living at this time.

On August 28, 1900, the Pikes Peak Daily News ran the following: Dr. Harriet A. Leonard, the oldest established physician in Manitou. all forms of chronic and nervous diseases treated successfully by

Dr. Leonard's original method
of administering dry electricity.
Office 122 Canon Avenue, Manitou.
Consultation free.

After a fall, in which she broke
her femur, Harriet's health declined.
she died in September of 1907.

Perhaps this piece from the Pueblo
Weekly Chieftain from April 27,
1876, will add some additional
insight into Dr. Harriet A. Leonard
and her journey to be a respected
doctor.

"There seems to be something the
matter with the doctors up here.
Dr. Harriet A. Leonard, the lady who
runs a vapor bath establishment,
things some of the other doctors

have been imposing upon her.
two or three articles appeared
in the 'avalanche' that were not
especially to the good lady's credit.
not the doctress [sic] comes back
with a letter of explanation and
accounts for the death of George
Thomas, one of her vapor bath
patients in a plausible manner.
vapor baths may be good for
an iron constitution, encased in a
heavy coating of mother earth; but
for narrow chested consumptives,
hanging on the brink of eternity,
one good strong vapor bath is
enough to take what little steam
out of them that may exist in their
flickering tenements.

Martha F. Miller - Headstone

Martha F. Miller

Block 64

Martha F. Miller

MARTHA **F**RANCES **M**ILLER WAS born on April 15, 1864, in Renssaleur County, New York. A search of the Ancestry records shows a large family.

Dr. Miller arrived in Colorado Springs in 1894 two years after graduating from medical school in New York. She took up residence at 217 Nevada Ave. By 1896 her older sister Jane, and two brothers, James and Ira, had joined her in Colorado Springs. The family lived at 4 Boulder Crescent in a boarding house that Jane ran. In the 1900 census, Jane is listed as owning the boarding house.

Jane was born in February 1851. Brother James, a builder, was born in May 1862, and Ira, a bookkeeper, and the youngest son was born in Delaware in October 1870. There also appears to be a sister Agnes, birth date unknown. Records regarding their early family life are sketchy.

In 1892 she graduated from the New York Hospital and Medical

College for Women. The college was incorporated by a special act of the legislature of New York in 1863. The college founder, Dr. Clemence Sophia Lozier fought for the right of women to not only attend medical school but she was also involved with women's suffrage and abolition.

By the time Dr. Miller graduated in 1893, the school had graduated two hundred and twenty women, physicians, and surgeons. The history of the school states that Emily Schettler was the first woman to graduate and was also the first woman in the United States to receive a medical diploma from a woman's medical college.

She remained in New York after graduation and was at 157 W 44th Street in 1893 according to the "The North American Journal of Homeopathy – 1893".

Dr. Miller continued her practice in Colorado Springs until 1910 when she removed to Seattle, Washington. There she ran a boarding house. Records indicate she discontinued her medical practice.

By 1940, at the age of 75, she was renting a home in Seattle for twenty dollars a month. She returned to Colorado Springs in 1950 and on

September 24, 1956, she died. She was 92 years old. According to her obituary, she was survived by a brother and sister, along with nieces and nephews.

Why Dr. Miller left the medical profession is unknown. Her obituary and headstone give no mention of her work in the medical field.

Minnie C. Coulter - Headstone

Minnie C. Coulter

Block 19-A

No headstone,

Resting between the two stones

Minnie C. Coulter

DR. **M**RS. **M**INNIE **C. Coulter** could be considered a bit of a mystery, even her final resting place isn't marked.

According to the 1900 census, Minnie was born in January 1833 in Germany. That same census indicated she'd been in the United States for fifty-six years and was a naturalized citizen. She moved around the country eventually ending her travels in Colorado Springs late in life. What her maiden name was is unknown at this time.

Minnie and her husband, George, appear in the 1880 Atchison, Kansas, City Directory, bedding in the Seitz Hotel. Additionally, that same directory shows twenty-nine physicians of which two are women.

Minnie and George remained in Atchison living at 612 Kansas Ave. In the 1885 census, George is listed as a journalist while Minnie's listing is physician.

An ad in the February 1, 1887, Atchison Daily Globe indicates the type of medicine Dr. Coulter practiced. It read: "Dr. Minnie Coulter No. 117 North Second St. between Commercial St. and Kansas Ave, does general practice but makes a specialty of chronic diseases."

In the November 14, 1887, the Atchison Daily Globe ran the following: "George S. Coulter, who represented this paper on the road until his fatal illness began, died at 3 o'clock yesterday afternoon, of consumption. His remains were sent to his old home in Davenport, Iowa, for his burial." This is probably Minnie's husband for the next directory listing, she is listed as widowed.

Mary De Mund, in her book, "Women Physicians of Colorado" wrote that Minnie Coulter was licensed to practice in Colorado in 1890. She wasn't a medical college graduate, nor did she have a degree. She received her license for her over ten years of medical experience. De Mund also states the Minnie started her medical practice in Pueblo. That information has yet to be verified.

We do know that she was in Leadville, Colorado, from 1894-1895 according to the city directory. She was the only woman doctor listed of the twenty-two in 1894 and the twenty-four in 1895.

Dr. Coulter appears in the 1898 Colorado Springs, City Directory, with an address of 317 N, Tejon St. She continued here in Colorado Springs until her death on August 25, 1902, on a trip to Lincoln, Nebraska.

Dr. Coulter's 'obituary' from the September 25, 1902, Colorado Springs Gazette:

"FUNERAL TODAY — Funeral services of the late Dr. M. Coulter will take place this afternoon at 3 o'clock from the late residents, No.11 East Boulder street. Dr. Coulter died in Omaha and the funeral was to have taken place yesterday but was postponed on account of the train bearing the remains being delayed."

In her sixty-nine years, Dr. Minnie C. Coulter traveled and always followed her profession, no matter where she was.

Hannah Taylor Muir - Headstone

Hannah Taylor Muir

Block 77

Chapter Sixteen

Hannah Taylor Muir

HANNAH **L**OUISE **T**AYLOR **M**UIR born in November 1859, died on November 4, 1926, of bronchopneumonia

Dr. Muir is probably most well known in Colorado Springs for her years as the doctor on staff at Colorado College. She followed Dr. Grace Preston, the first woman to hold that position, after Dr. Preston's departure.

The students appear to respect and like her. Her name appears at various times in the college newspaper. Once they mention how much they are glad she is back after traveling to Philadelphia and staying for several months for her health. In another mention, the piece states "Dr. Muir is back again and there is great rejoicing over the fact. Some of the young ladies have shown their appreciation by getting sick."

Born in Pennsylvania to William and Jane Taylor. According to the 1870 census her parents were born in

Ireland. She had three brothers, two older and one younger. At that time her father was working as a railroad clerk.

Dr. Muir graduated from the Woman's Medical College in Pennsylvania in 1890. She was a clinical obstetrician, at the University of Colorado, 1893-95. The Assistant County physician of Arapahoe County in Colorado from 1893-94. She took post-graduate courses at the School of Medicine and Polyclinic in New York in 1895, the Allgmein Polyclinic in Vienna in 1896, and Philadelphia Polyclinic in 1897 after taking the position at Colorado College in 1895. While at Colorado College she was the instructor in hygiene and a medical advisor.

The three polyclinics Dr. Muir attended were some of the top such clinics at the time. Polyclinics offered medical services to the public, along with diverse specialties under one umbrella. These specialties also offered classes to further education for medical doctors.

Dr. Muir's original medical college, founded in 1850, is said to be the first medical institution in the world established for the instruction and training of women to attain an M.D. Degree.

Hannah Louise Taylor married Dr. James T. Muir on April 2, 1896, in Colorado Springs. Her address while at Colorado College was 611 N. Tejon Street, Colorado Springs, CO. There were no children from the marriage.

Her husband, James (1857-1928) was also a doctor. He'd been born in India and immigrated to the US in 1879.

Anna Shaw Chamberlain - Headstone

Anna Chamberlain

Block 74

Anna Shaw Chamberlain

ANNA **S**HAW **C**HAMBERLAIN, DDS was born in Detroit, Michigan in 1866. By the time Anna was thirteen, the family had moved to Harlan, Page County, Iowa. On September 1, 1886, in Page County, Iowa, at the age of twenty she married Frank C. Chamberlain. Frank was an 1884 Graduate of the University of Iowa – Dental

Department. The couple arrived in Colorado around 1887 when Anna was twenty-one.

Dr. Chamberlain has the honor of being in the first graduating class of the University of Denver's Dental School. In 1887 the University opted to begin a Dental College. Once a building was available in 1888 the Denver Dental College opened its doors and on April 3, 1889, the school graduated its first four students: Anna D. Chamberlain, A. Leonard Sanderson, E.W. Varley, and Wilber R. Wilson.

Dr. Chamberlain and her husband, Frank, were active in the community. In 1902, Frank was in on the beginning of the Dental Society in the region. The goal of the society was to grow the knowledge of the areas dentists with the presenting of papers and discussions.

Dr. Chamberlain was also active in the W.C.T.U. (Women's Christian Temperance Union) and was elected president of the Colorado Springs branch of the organization in 1897. This was in addition to her practice and raising the couple's two sons.

The celebration of Frank and Anna's twenty-fifth wedding anniversary, in 1911, was well attended according to the write-up in the local Colorado Springs newspaper.

In 1912 their son, Dean Chamberlain, graduated from dental school in Denver, following in his parent's footsteps. Later their son Paul F. Chamberlains, after serving in WWI, also became a dentist.

On April 30, 1914, Dr. Chamberlain died in her home surrounded by family. The official diagnosis was pernicious anemia.

A portion of the May 3, 1914 Gazette notice states:

"Dr. Chamberlain was a prominent dentist, and all dentists of the city will attend the funeral today in a body. "

Esther B. Holmes - Headstone

Esther B. Holmes

Block 53

She was buried right behind the stone

on the right.

Chapter Twenty

Esther B. Holmes

ESTHER **B. HOLMES** WAS originally buried in Evergreen, she was disinterred and reburied in Westville Cemetery in Taunton, Massachusetts. I've included Dr. Holmes for her time spent in Colorado Springs.

Esther Holmes arrived in Colorado Springs around 1879. She, along with Clara B. Rowe, Harriett

Leonard, and Julia Loomis, comprised the first four women physicians in the area.

Dr. Holmes came from Natik, Bristol, Rhode Island where she was born on April 15, 1843. She married George F. Holmes, age twenty-one, when she was fifteen, on December 26, 1858, in Mansfield, Massachusetts. Her maiden name was Winslow, daughter of Avery and Maria Winslow and the youngest of their six children.

Esther Holmes attended the Cleveland Women's Homeopathic College, graduating in 1871 at the age of twenty-seven or twenty-eight. The city directory from 1877 shows George and Esther living at 1062 Woodland Avenue in Cleveland, Ohio. George had a meat market at that address, along with Esther's practice.

In 1881 Colorado began licensing physicians, both male and female. Dr. Holmes received her license #387 in 1882. During her many years of practice in the Pikes Peak region, Dr. Holmes became known as 'The Baby Doctor'. Her husband, George, was involved in many endeavors, including mining, but was best known for his years in the shoe business.

In her later years, as her health was failing she lived with her nephew, Clarence A. Franklin, at 926 Cheyenne Rd., Colorado Springs.

Dr. Holmes passed on August 30, 1909, at the home of her nephew, Clarence A. Franklin. She was sixty-six years old. The cause of death is listed as a cerebral hemorrhage.

Chapter Twenty-One

Other Doctors in the Area

LEST YOU THINK THERE were only a few female physicians in Colorado Springs prior to the early 1900s, below is a list of women doctors, with short biographies, who are listed as physicians in the Colorado Springs, Colorado City, Manitou Springs City Directories for the years 1879-1900. Those listed started a practice here prior to moving to another area or perhaps deciding to leave the profession. Some came for their health, some to take part in Women's Suffrage, and some because the area was a health mecca.

<u>Clara Belle Rowe</u> – Born in Massachusetts in 1833, Clara was the fourth female physician to arrive in Colorado Springs by 1880. After the death of her husband, F..J. Rowe, a real estate agent, she moved to California. Like Esther B. Holmes and Julia E. Loomis, Dr. Rowe was an 1871 graduate of the Cleveland Women's Homeopathic College.

<u>Mary E Bryan</u> – Graduate of the Women's Medical College of Pennsylvania, she was in Colorado Springs before returning back east. She was also a missionary who spent many years in India. She died in April 1931.

<u>E. J. Wall</u> - This is probably Dr. Eliza J. Wall, an 1899 University Medical College Kansas City, Kansas City graduate. Dr. Wall was only in Colorado Springs for a brief time. She appears in the 1900 Denver City Directory along with her sister, Sarah, who was a nurse.

<u>E. A. Watts</u> – Eugenia A. Watts was born in 1847 in Illinois. She was an 1880 graduate of Northwestern

University Women's Medical School, Chicago: Women's Hospital Medical College. She applied for a California Medical License in 1880m giving her residence as La Jara, Colorado. The license was issued in 1884. Although in Colorado Springs in 1890, she also appears in the 1890 Polk Medical Directory as being in La Jara, Colorado. Her application in 1888 for her Colorado Medial License has her county as both El Paso and Conejos. In studying her history, it appears she worked in La Jara for at least ten years.

H.S. Carper - Mrs. Harriet Carper is not listed any other time than in the 1894 City Directory. She is listed as a physician along with her husband, Andrew J. Carper. After leaving this region it appears the couple returned to Indiana where Andrew continued his practice. Harriet returned to Colorado Springs around 1910 and is listed as living with her son. At the time of Andrew's death, Harriett was in Colorado Springs but returned to Indiana for the funeral. The reason for her return to Colorado Springs has not been located as of this writing.

Helen T. Myers – Graduated from Hahnemann medical college in 1883. Prior to her arrival in Colorado Springs, she had a practice in the

San Diego, California area. Once she arrived in Colorado Springs Dr. Myers remained for a number of years. While here she invested in mines and applied for a patent for a refrigerator. She died in 1916 in Falconer, New York. Practiced in the San Diego, CA., area in 1889-1890.

Grace A Preston – Dr. Preston graduated in 1890 from the Women's Medical College in New York. She was on staff at Smith College and was the one who advised Florence Sabin to study in the medical field. Dr. Preston was the first female resident physician at Colorado College from 1893 to 1895 after moving to Colorado

Springs for her 'lung troubles'. She moved on to Southern California. She died there at the age of thirty-six.

Sarah Ellis – Born in Virginia in 1830. Like Minnie Coulter, she was licensed by the state of Colorado in 1894, without graduating from a medical college although she did take classes at the Homeopathic Hospital and College in Cleveland, OH.

Greene, Dr. Mrs. - There has been no record found of this person other than their one-time appearance in the Colorado Springs City Directory.

<u>Idella Fagaley</u> – Dr. Fagaley was born in Missouri in 1865. She was a graduate of the Southwestern Homeopathic Medical College and Hospital in Louisville, Kentucky. She was licensed in Kentucky in 1896 and then in Colorado in 1898. She started her practice in Louisville, Kentucky, taking over the practice of Dr. Clara Plimpton.

<u>Mary H. Platt</u> – Dr. Platt was born in 1860 in Philadelphia, Pennsylvania. She was an 1891 graduate of the Philadelphia Medical College of Pennsylvania. She died in 1899 and is buried in Pennsylvania.

<u>Sarah J Springer</u> – Dr. Springer was an eclectic physician. Her husband, civil war veteran Stephen H Springer, lived a number of years in Colorado Springs, but Sarah appears to have discontinued her medical practice after 1900.

Mary A. Lutz – Mary Alice Lutz only appears in the 1900 Colorado City Directory. She was a graduate of the University of Nebraska class of 1886. She is listed in their 1923 list of graduates, but her address is unknown. One source puts her birth date as 1878, but it is far more likely that the date is 1858-1860 in the state of Iowa.

Josephine L. Peavey – in 1898 Dr. Peavey was secretary/treasurer of the Denver Clinical Society. In 1906 she was the president of the Board of Directors of the Girls' Industrial School in Colorado Springs. By 1909 she was representing the El Paso County Medical Society at the Public Health Education Committee.

<u>Alice Beverleigh</u> – While little has been found in Colorado about Dr. Beverleigh, in 1889 there is a Dr. Alice M. Beverleigh who is the manager of the Beverleigh Manufacturing Company in Seattle, Washington. While it may be a different person, the unique spelling of the name would indicate they are the same.

<u>Mary F. Brenton</u> - Dr. Mary Foster Brenton was born in 1858 in New York. She attended and graduated from the University of Michigan Medical School in Ann Arbor, Michigan. She graduated in 1885 and was married to William H. Brenton in Michigan that same year. According to the book "Colorado Healthcare Heritage", Mary Brenton was in Green Mountain Falls in 1888 with her engineer husband. It was said she would treat those who came to her for free. By 1900 she was practicing her craft in Colorado Springs. She died in 1934 in Palo Alto, California.

Anne P. Holt – Anne Prosser was born in Tennessee in 1871. In 1891 she married H. Clay Holt. She graduated from Tufts University of Medicine in Boston, Massachusetts, in 1898. She was licensed in 1900 in Colorado. In 1901 she married Carl E. Trulock from Chicago. She died in New Jersey in 1908 of anemia.

Fannie C. Cooper – Dr. Fannie C. Cooper was born on November 23, 1871, in Kansas. She died in Los Angles, California, on November 28, 1945. She was married to F. M. Cooper, also a doctor. The couple had a practice in Manitou Springs. In 1930 the couple were living in Washougal, Clark County, Washington where her husband Francis M. died. The couple had two children, Margaret and Elizabeth.

<u>Caroline E. Spencer</u> – Dr. Spencer was born in 1862 in Pennsylvania and was an 1892 graduate of the Women's Medical College of Pennsylvania. She was licensed in Pennsylvania in 1892 and then in 1893 in Colorado. She is probably best remembered for her participation in the National Women's Party and their fight for women's suffrage here in the West and on the National level.

Chapter Twenty-Two

About The Author

ABOUT THE AUTHOR

Doris A. McCraw is a mid-westerner who found her home at the foot of Pikes Peak in the Rocky Mountains of Colorado. As a child, she would sit and listen to the stories of those around her. It was the beginning of a lifelong passion to find and share the stories of those who preceded her.

The midwest where she grew up was filled with stories of pioneers who braved the wilderness to build forts, towns, and businesses. The Mississippi River, near her hometown, also inspired a love of nature.

Once she arrived in Colorado the plains, mountains, and the adventurers who traveled through reinforced her love of the stories of the people who made history. Once she found the obituary of Julia E. Loomis she began a journey to tell the stories of these early women physicians who gave so much. It became her mission to make sure their names were not forgotten.

Her poetry and fiction writing also came from history. As Helen (Hunt) Jackson she learned a new appreciation for the world around her. It also inspired Doris to pursue publication to continue to share her passion for the world around her.

Chapter Twenty-Three

Additional Reading – Bibliography

1879- 1900 Colorado Springs City Directories

"Doctor's, Disease, and Dying", Tim Blevins- editor.

"A Parting Address." Cleveland Daily Herald, 3 Mar. 1870. Nineteenth Century U.S. Newspapers.

"Colorado's Healthcare Heritage", Tom Sherlock

"Women Physicians of Colorado", Mary De Mund

"History of Buchanan County, Iowa: 1842-1881", Williams Bros. Publishers

Directory of Deceased Physicians – Ancestry.com

"New Woodstock and Vicinity Past and Present", Mary E. Richmond

"A Century of Colorado Medicine 1871-1971", Harvey T. Sethman, editor

"Colorado Physicians License Applications 1881-1967", Gerald E. Sherard

"Colorado Medicine. Vol. 3",
Colorado State Medical Society,
1906

"New Woodstock and Vicinity,
Past and Present", Ellsworth and
Richmond

Chapter Twenty-Four

Note Page

THANK YOU FOR READING, **"Under the Stone"**. This is the first book in telling the stories of the Women Doctors who practiced their profession in Colorado prior to 1900. If you enjoyed and found the information useful, please share it with others who also have a thirst for knowledge.

Additionally, please use this page for notes and questions. Feel free to contact ChinookMountainPublishing@gmail.com if you wish more information, have questions about these amazing women, or wish to book an In-person or Zoom presentation.